Pearl Blac
Painted Silks:
The Language of Fans

Leena Batchelor

Pearl Blades and Painted Silks:
The Language of Fans

Leena Batchelor

Edited by Black Pear Press

First published in 2021 by Black Pear Press

www.blackpear.net

Copyright © Leena Batchelor

ISBN 978-1-913418-47-2

Cover Photograph by Suz Winspear
Cover Design by Leena Batchelor and Black Pear Press

Black Pear Press

Madam de Staël (1766-1817):

"What grace does not a fan place at a woman's disposal if she only knows how to use it properly! It waves, it flutters, it closes, it expands, it is raised or lowered according to circumstances. Oh! I will wager that in all the paraphernalia of the loveliest and best-dressed women in the world, there is no ornament with which she can produce so great an effect."

A Personal Thank You

Pearl Blades and Painted Silks: The Language of Fans

It would be impossible for me to say 'thanks' to everyone who has inspired me, that would be a book in itself, but know that you, the reader, the casual observer, are one of the many who have provided the ingredients for this smörgåsbord. Viewing life through the nib of a pen allows me the indulgence of committing experiences to sheaves of written parchment as quickly as the moments that created them flee by. However, I would like to draw attention to certain noteworthy individuals without whom this particular collection would have remained in the filing cabinets of my mind instead of upon your bookshelves:

Worcestershire LitFest & Fringe for appointing me as their Worcestershire Poet Laureate 2020-21—I'm still not convinced they knew what they were unleashing!

Black Pear Press for their invaluable advice and support during the conception and birth of the much-loved creation you now hold.

Everyone in the Worcester Spoken Word community who seven years ago welcomed a novice poet and helped her literary flower to grow.

Jules Davies and Suz Winspear for allowing me insight into their personal fan collections and proving that the language of fans is still well and truly alive!

And finally, to my English grandmother, Ruby Doris Bayliss (1899-1975), for fuelling my imagination and indulging my love of history and fantasy.

Dedicated to

a dearly missed friend and mentor: Kieran Davis—a weaver of words,

and for my beautiful children, Tanya, Max, Emma, Liam—always in my heart and thoughts, my raison d'être.

Without you all, the whispers of my soul could not fly

19th century Japanese fan

Why a Poetry Collection about Fans?

I remember being fascinated by them since a young child. My English grandmother allowed me to play dress-up from her amazing wardrobe full of beautiful fans, silk Chinese dresses, and lace Victorian outfits, fuelling my child's imagination. This later led to my love of all things Steampunk, combining my fascination with Victoriana, fantastical inventions, and my forays among the science fiction writings of Asimov, E.E. 'Doc' Smith and Heinlein secreted from my father's bookshelves. In my teens I discovered the dark sophistication of Lovecraft and Poe, resulting in a very unconventional English Lit student. Little wonder many of my teachers despaired! These imaginings were played out in her beautiful home backing onto the flowing waters of the Thames, just yards from Hampton Court Palace and across the road from Bushy Park; a veritable playground for any child wishing to lose herself among the weavings of time.

Sadly, these wonderful *objet fantastique* have since been lost following her death when I was just nine years old; memories, however, stay forever. Outwardly, my grandmother was quite particular about etiquette and proper behaviour in society, but our private moments together enabled me to glean something magical from her stories and weave them into my own lucid daydreams.

Today, with climate change and ever warmer summers, these beautiful devices are once again becoming popular and practical ways of keeping us cool while looking elegant; they have also been popularised as a formal form in T'ai Chi.

Now, several decades later, as Worcestershire Poet Laureate, I can write this daydream anthology. My aspiration was to write a collection of poems about the language of fans, but as is usual with the thought-hamsters running amok in my mind, research has taken me down many varied directions and has developed into so much more than a discourse on the vernacular of lace and veiled fluttering.

This collection is divided into two parts; the first presents fans across ages and continents, with interesting excerpts and images uncovered during my research, and a smattering of childhood recollections and multifarious poems; the second presents the story of the 1860s lady from debutante to dowager through the language of her fans. For miscellany there is also a glossary of fan types at the end.

Enjoy!

Vintage black & red fan, paper leaf with wood sticks c1950; from the author's collection

Contents

Illustrations
Part 1—Multifarious, Historical, and Reflective

Title	Illustration	Page
Japanese Fan	20th-c Japanese fan	Cover
Japanese Fan	19th-c Japanese fan	v
Queen of Fans	Mid-20th-c polka dot fan	1
Zephyr	19th-c Chinese fan	4
Komori	20th-c Japanese fan	6
Samurai Blades	19th-c Japanese fan	8
Dancer	20th-c sequined fan	11
Bess's Swan	Early-20th-c feather fan	14
Courtly Etiquette XIV	20th-c Mallorca fan	16
Cabaret at Moulin Rouge	20th-c sequined fan	20
España	20th-c Spanish fan	26
Tales of an Elephant	19th-c mica Burmese fan	28
Forever Sister	20th-c Japanese fan	30

Part 2—The 1860s Lady

Title	Illustration	Page
The Season	20th-c wooden fan	31
Cupid's Messenger	20th-c hand-painted Spanish fan	33
Discourse	20th-c wooden fan	36
Dowager	20th-c lace fan	37
The Poet	Leena Batchelor	41

Part 1—Multifarious, Historical, and Reflective

Queen of Fans

Churches in the Dark Ages used fans as liturgical objects, the most famous being Queen Theodelinda's fan, a 6ᵗʰ century fan preserved in the treasury at the Cathedral at Monza, along with her crown, comb and golden hens. This indomitable regent directly influenced many of the important political and religious arguments of the day; a testament to the fact that women have for centuries, and behind the scenes, been empowered.

contd…

That Queen of Lombardy,
Waved her fan to disseminate 'twixt faiths of Nicene and Arian;
Waved the burning coals from the burial of her first love;
(Oh, alas! Dear Authari!)
Waved her fan and chose her second;
(Welcome darling Agilulf!)
Chaffed by the winds of politics to welcome Byzantine bribes,
Theodelinda, Lombardy Queen,
Theodelinda, woman supreme,
Waved her fan to clear her path,
Waved her fan to make her mark.

By Parchment Veiled

The Chinese and Japanese were among the first innovators of fan use. The most common fan in early China was the screen fan (pien-mien), used by modest girls when out in society.

I wish to hide,
My visage is not one for you to look upon,
I am not free.
I offer you a painted scene,
For maiden modesty,
An embroidered reflection of my story—
The fishing heron awaiting its catch,
Beautified ribbons of water beneath webbed feet.

I wish to hide,
My visage is one for you to wait upon.

Zephyr

Zephyrs were modesty screens of fans used by both sexes in Roman baths.

The breath of an entrance behind the screen, naked blushes
  hidden from leering stares as disembodied shapes reveal
  through the steam,
Shy gazes upon a statuesque Adonis as his gaze alights upon the
  painted vellum,
Does he dream of the wonders hiding there, beneath the blue
  eyed stare?
Will a painted delight fall from the screen, fold, as his resolve
  surely must once she is seen, in daylight, clothed, seeming
  serene?
Or will she meld once more back into the steam, anonymous to
  everyone before the screen?

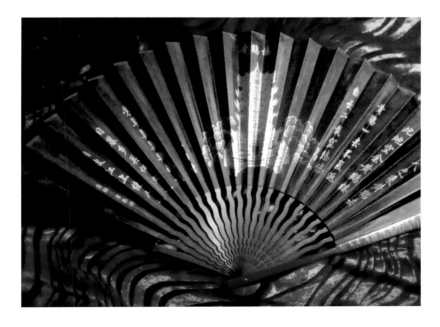

Saracen Sunset

Noted by the Crusaders for the painted designs upon their war fans, the Saracen ideas were brought back and became de rigueur for the shields of English chivalric knights.

The blood-red tribal cries of a thousand fans captured our
    eyeline, shrilled through our ears, and fed our swords as their
    life cried into the sands.

A panoply of colour arose with Saracen sun only to be charged
    down; we believed them wrong, their beliefs of science and
    difference, denied them existence, and stole their ideals home.

Our devices then coloured and charged with a nation's religion,
    taken for our own. Frippery now for romances of chivalry.

Invasion. Theft. History bereft.

A wandering cry still dusts Saracen sunsets.

Komori

Named after the Japanese folding fans—also the Japanese for 'bat' which inspired the design of these fans. As a culture, the Japanese have always been in tune with nature and many of their designs arise from this.

Such an emblem of life is not to be ignored.
The birth from the central rivet, holding tight and secure,
Safe.
Growth from the expansion of bamboo sticks towards leaves
of
Calligraphy parchment, life's journals inscribed upon the road
of breezes whispered by
Komori.

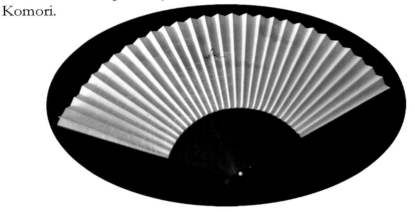

While the fan remains open,
Prosperity promised in perpetuity

Promises kept.

While the fan rests closed.
Safety. Growth. Continuity.

Life's gifts offered to the open mind.

Folded Songs

In the Chinese Song Dynasty (960–1279) it is written that the Japanese monk Chonen gifted folding fans to the emperor of China in 988, making this the earliest record of a folding fan, and probably an original invention by the Japanese.

Sing me a song, sing me a song,
Of days that are long gone.
Sing me a song, sing me a song,
From wrist to hand to sky.
Unfurl me, open me,
Let me sing to thee
Across crowded rooms
Of desire and dreams.

It lies hidden, at rest, but never idle, this bard of the hand.
Turtle-shell adorned in whimsy, a fête of capering moons across
starlit lands,
Turquoise peacockery on edges laced,
A handle broad with bejewelled face.

Unfurled and awake, it sings.
It calls to dust motes to vacate an empress' state,
It calls to maidens keeping chaste.
Painted songs of empire, life and love so great
The coldest of hearts become tender, their ice walls break.

Sing me a song, painted herald, sing me a song,
Sing to me, painted herald, sing to me.

Samurai Blades

Historically, Japanese hand fans were tools of aristocrats and the Samurai class, who had their own selection of iron war fans.

I gaze at the case in the museum, and my eyes see the rusted pivots and rotted blades of iron, while my heart vibrates to the beats of the songs whispered across Time's ears.

I wonder at the hands that held such devices, objects of famed desire and death, reflections of myself upon the glass carefully placed as if holding the precious items displayed.

I hear the calls of both armour and paramour. Bladed shields of iron, azure paint and gold, striking fear upon the faces of foes and desire in the hearts of lovers doe-eyed.

I step away, releasing the breath held in awe of a terrifying beauty, vapourising on the glass as Time drifts into shimmers of history upon Samurai blades.

A Pauper's Offering

Farmers winnowed precious cereals from their grains using a 'fann'. Many English heraldic devices feature winnowing fans—notably Richard Coeur de Lion and the Earl of Arundel, Edward III.

I will winnow, m'lord, and I will sweat,
The chaff and grain no more together set.
In the fields, harvest-gathering,
In the sun, the heat is slavering,
Bodies wilt in dry soil as they toil
All for m'lord's tithes and spoils.

I will winnow, m'lord, and as I sweat,
When your eyes no longer upon me set,
Unfurl my fann and excite air to my brow
So under the sun's heat I do not cower.

When Time arrives to winnow you, m'lord,
Separate you from the chaff of the living world,
Will you have my fann sculpted,
Forever impressed
Within your family sepulchre,
While my body wilts in dry unmarked soil
All for your tithes and spoils?

Allegorical

Early fans depicted hand-painted biblical allegories, but the onset of the eighteenth century saw the development of the printed fan: cheaper to manufacture, making fans available to a much wider audience than previously. Equally, the variety of subjects depicted on fan leaves became increasingly varied, reflecting contemporary preoccupations and pastimes.

According to the scripture, parables in pearl, painted upon
    sheaves of vellum, holy writ was learned.
According to the market place, parables of games, printed en
    mass for the mass of material gain.
Crying of churches losing ground, how to spread the word?
Crying of factories, how much have they earned?
Who reads the works, who sees the subliminal message, what
    does this change presage?
Who can we entice, who will pay the price, what does this
    change presage?

Faces evolve as tales are retold, fans revolve in history's turning
    doors.

Dancer

French Fans in the 18th and 19th centuries became incredibly intricately detailed and designed, created from exotic materials such as bone, ivory, tortoiseshell, silk, and mother-of-pearl, and garnished with appliqué, brocade threads, lace, tulle, silhouette cutting, engraving, metallic foil finishes, wash drawing, and gilding.

She danced shadows across the moonlit floor, a musical of
    peacock turquoise and emerald green.
Left step, then right, twirl then hold,
Feathery offerings from gracious wrists, oh, so bold!
Candle-flame reflections softly pirouette,
    a shimmering litany to accompany the feminine silhouettes,
In the dance of the shadows across the moonlit floor.

Elocution and Flirtation

Jean-Pierre Duvelleroy was a Parisian fan maker. In 1827 he distributed a booklet with his fans that was regarded as the first manual of fan language. Whilst this may have been a marketing ploy, many authors made reference to the power of a fan in a lady's hand, which suggests that ladies wielded their fans with a purpose.

Beauty adorned; the value of the message diffused by fluttering
  hands,
These ornaments and their uses.
The dainty Japanese that ripples intent,
The coquetry of the Spanish flamenco twisting in the wrist.
Dignity, grace and reticence join hands to reveal
Romance and statement.
These painted, flighty embellishments with simple agitation can
  exile a hopeful heart
Or betray the yearning of one such.

The wise maiden, the hopeful spinster,
The advantageous, the flirtatious,
All display and shade their thoughts for the unsuspecting.

The games of polite society, ego fanning and candle blowing,
The debutante balls, showers of fine white lace and linen
  bedewing the trill of conversation,
Held with gloves and pearls translucent among diamond
  chandeliers.

The lover becomes a reed in the hands of the one who uses her
  fan with skill,
Pliable and playing her tune,
But only when playing society's rules.

Bess's Swan

Elizabeth I was a keen user of fans who popularised their presence in England. Many jewel encrusted, white feather fans were given as gifts by her admirers, among them Robert Dudley and Sir Francis Drake. Just before she died, her household inventory included 27 fans. In 1588, her close friend the Countess of Bath is recorded as having given her:

> *a fanne of swannes down, with a maze of gilene velvet, ymbroidered with seed pearles and a very small chayne of silver gilte, and in the midst a border on both sides of seed pearles, sparkes of rubyes and emerods, and thereon a monster of gold, the head and breast mother-of-pearls*

My dearest Countess, your treasure I
hold dear against my breast.

The gentlest breeze of swan down
kisses my cheek, and pearl tears
hold the seeds of recalled sorrow,
and joy.

Such an elegance of emerald
cabochons recall *his* eyes as he once
gazed upon me; do you remember
how we danced the firelight, him
and me?

How you said our trysts were held in your trust?

Oh, his sweet grace as he brushed my fingertips across his lips,
as I now brush the swan down across mine.

You and I alone know.
You and I alone.

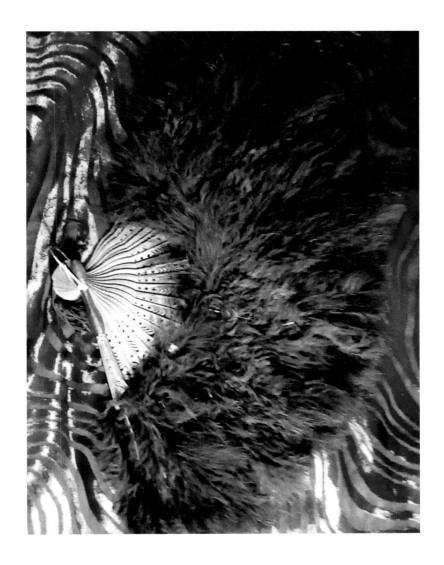

Courtly Etiquette XIV

In 17th century France, masquerade balls using fans became elaborate rituals of flirtation; in the court of Louis XIV they were an essential accessory. Court etiquette dictated that fans had to remain closed in the presence of the King, leading to the handles becoming more and more elaborately decorated. The placement and use of a fan would determine your ranking in the French court.

Women blush, dissembling embarrassed airs and timidity,
Women blush, hiding painted faces behind duplicity.
Painted veils of lace and pearl remain furled,
Where fans once flirted now gemstone handles hold courtly
    rule.

Women blush, dissembling attitudes for all to see,
Women blush, cochineal rouge highlighting false beauty.
A shoulder tapped, a palm struck, but no smile hidden
    modestly,
In this French court of etiquette, the king must view everyone's
    set.

Left, or right, to the side, allow the king the choice to toy,
He will have the say in this fanned court of intrigue and ploy.

Elocutionary Execution

Inspired by a satirical piece from The Spectator published in 1711 after noting that fans were recognised in society as a method for surreptitious communication.

> *"Woman are armed with Fans as Men with Swords, and sometimes do more Execution with them...I have seen a Fan so very angry that it would have been dangerous for the absent Lover who provoked it to have come within the Wind of it; and at other times so very languishing, that I have been glad for the Lady's sake that the Lover was at a sufficient Distance from it."*

They hold the balance of desire and distress within their palms, these ladies and their devices. Men with their swords are no match for the rapiers of wit and savagery that exudes from these belles and their fans.

One turn of a wrist, a man will fall upon his knees, whether from acceptance of his courtship or denial of his suit.

The lady will at once dissemble, be both bashful, timorous in demeanour and coquette, eager to engage.

Beware, young man, the lady and her fan.
Beware, young man, execution by parchment elocution.

Lure of the Laced Lover

Inspired by Soame Jenyn's 'The Art of Dancing' (1729).

I am the trap, the wanton lure.
Dare not embark with a free hand or unveiled face into society's
    abyss-dark dance.
Prepare for the war,
A mighty fluttering of plumed embellishment against and for
    the male intent,
Learn my semaphore.

Your gaze, as it pores upon the blades held firm by ringed
    fingers,
Whether in abject desolation or the throes of flamed desire,
Will call to the peacocked dandies across the ballroom floor
And draw them in to your trap.

Your secret shame I will hide,
Your anger at presumption I will display.
I will be your shield,
I will be your swain.

My lexicon is yours to unveil at will.
My trap is yours to spring.

Cabaret at Moulin Rouge

Enormous ostrich plumed fans were used to discreetly cover the stars of the Moulin Rouge, and can still be seen today on the variety and burlesque stages worldwide.

At the cabaret, such a display, fans galore to hide shame and
    allude with modesty
Enticing enticements.
Slow, elegant, fluttering displays languor across the stage with
    listless beauty,

Until the tempo change;

Then within the whirr of a tornado vivacity comes alive.

Mistinguett dances with Chevalier,
Burlesque poses in shadows and lights,
Magical instruments expressing conceits as subtle as the
    butterfly's kiss upon a summer's breeze,
Or the most unreasonable of demands upon its audience.

The cabaret, modesty veiled by immodest fans.

Fanned Therapy

Harking back to their Asiatic origins, fans are recognised as a form in Fan T'ai Chi, a graceful martial art providing contemplation and poise.

Grace gathers and

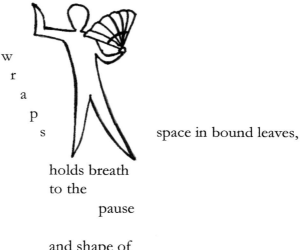

w

r

a

p

s   space in bound leaves,

holds breath
to the
          pause

and shape of
calm.

Entranced in meditation, a distraction of beauty enters the mind As easily as the kingfisher *swoops* across   ribbons   of   air currents.

The beauty alone is disarming, alluring in its artistry and delicacy, belies the strength and power thrumming through the silk and blades.
Concealment and diversion becomes its own weapon through form and dance, style and elegance.

Yet the weapon also heals; calms ripples across surfaces of dyed silk.   contd…

Focused poise dams the noise of life, pulls the flow of settled space into limbs and breathing heartbeats,

Then folds and rests upon blades of steel.

Dance

Another childhood memory from my grandmother's fans.

We danced, you and I,
Across the floor and onto moonlit terraces.
We danced, you and I,
Into visions of elegance and time.
We danced, you and I,
Bequeathed a sheaving of memory,
The articulation of whispered winds upon sight.

We danced, you and I,
Among the kisses of midnight.

Grandma

My English grandmother, although a seemingly austere lady, was the one who introduced me to my love of fans and dress-up. She died just after my ninth birthday, and sadly her beautiful collection of fans has since been lost.

Me aged seven, playing dress-up from your wardrobe in childish
  delight.
Chinese silk, embroidered red and rich, nestled among
Victorian lace and mahogany shadows
Rustled in my child's hands.
I am a princess, being chased by dragons.
I am a princess; I must play chaste.
And then there they were, precious and precocious within their
  parchment linings, fluttering delights of fancy.
Dare I touch, dare I?
May I touch, may I?
The princess within grew regal, elegant;
But only while veiled behind the feathers and painted silks.

Me aged nine, playing dress-up one last time, childish no more.
Elegance in hand, scents of memory in my heart, embroidery of
  time woven in my hair.
I held the silk against my lips, kissed the times I had there with
  you,
And opened the parchment lined box of childish imaginings
  once more.

Me in my recollection years, wishing for the games of dress-up
  to escape life's brutality and time-hop back to innocence.
The follies of feathered fans, crusades of Chinese silk,
  voraciousness of Victorian lace.
I am a princess once more, regal and elegant;
But only while veiled behind childhood memories.

España

When relatives in my family travelled, they would return with souvenirs for the curious child left behind. Among my treasures is a small Spanish fan.

A memento of a visit I never had, yet hold the memory in my
  hand.
I walk the streets of España,
My child's eyes awake to the passion of flamenco and tastes of
  tapas,
My child's hand safe in your grown-up palm.

There but not there,
I walk the streets of España,

With the wave of a fan, my now folds its leaves, nestles against
  fretted blades and life dances as my mind is freed,
while
I walk the streets of España.

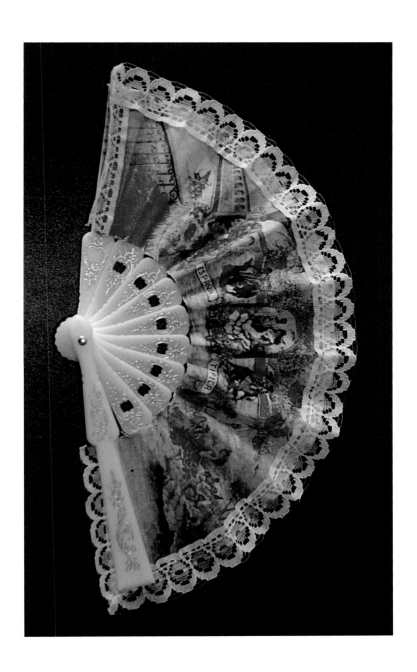

Tales of an Elephant

In Asia, the blades of many fans would be made from intricately carved ivory, polished by rubbing them with pumice stone and water.

They sang, his memories; skimming through her fingers as the blades slid against the pumice. Water dripped onto sun-baked mud as the dual swish and rub of wet against rough smoothed away the tales of the elephant whose face had been adorned by these jewels. Once polished, sheened into nothingness, the glistening blades would be intricately carved, the jeweller's saw fretting to create frozen lace, crocheted from solid ivory, shavings floating away in the gentle Byzantine breeze; a life forgotten, a new one to begin.

The diamond edge circled upon the tip of each, danced its vicious bite into, then through, the finery of wafered tusk. One more hole into the mineral memory of majesty. Sheaves of parchment bore the calligraphy of painted history, tales of the blades' forbearer caught in frozen mid-step, only dancing when conjoined with ribbon to obey the elocution of the wrist.

Lying upon the parched soil, dusted by time and tumbleweed, the elephant told his final story, the death throes of stolen majesty, while his anonymous tusks danced among chandeliers and lace.

Forever Sister

This is the darker side of fan language and deserves a full explanation. Nushu was a language devised in China, notably the Jiangyong province, as the world's sole 'women only' language. The story has since been popularised in a book called 'Snow Flower and the Secret Fan' by Lisa See, and made into a film in 2011 starring Hugh Jackman.

In 19th century China, girls were forever bonded together as sworn sisters (laotong) by a matchmaker to ease the pain of isolation and provide emotional companionship and encourage ideals of eternal fidelity, while they awaited their marriages. Isolated by their families, they communicated by writing in a secret language on a unique fan.

One day in the 1960s, an old woman fainted in a rural Chinese train station. When the police searched her belongings in an effort to identify her, they came across papers written with what appeared to be a secret code. The woman was arrested and detained on suspicion of being a spy. When the scholars who came to decipher the code realised it was not something related to international intrigue, but rather a written language used solely by women which had been kept a 'secret' from men for a thousand years, they were promptly sent to a labour camp and detained for nearly 20 years. Now the study of Nushu is allowed by the People's Republic of China in recognition of its importance to its people's history.

Sadly, few original Nushu documents have survived.

We were scared.
Sacred Sisters.
We were scared.

We held our troth to our
Sacred Sisters;
We held our troth.

Chinese ink,
Parchment painted calligraphy,

contd…

Silken sleeves.

They could never know,
Those who held our bonds.
They would never know.

They observed, but did not see us,
Those who held our bonds.
They heard, but did not listen to us.

Bound feet,
Bound lives,
Free spirits.

I made my vows to you, sister.
Forever now my sister.
You made your vows to me, sister.

Open hearts inscribed upon open fans,
Closed to those who must not know the truth of our minds.
Open hearts bonded, bounded, inscribed within secrecy.

Sisters exchanging fans as fathers exchange their daughters.

We were scared.
Sacred Sisters, and yet
We were together,

Sacred Sisters,
Forever Sisters.

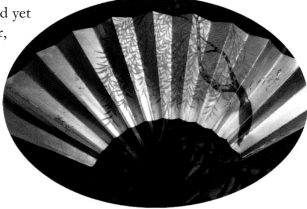

Part 2—The 1860's Lady

The Season

I am of age, my coming out ball. A year older from my sweet
    sixteen self, a year no wiser of what lies ahead.

Cocktail parties and dances abound, dresses and fans and veils
    and shoes to be found, and bound,
Tight with ribbon and etiquette to form sylph silhouettes.

I am primed, taught,
I will be the epitome of that which I ought,

For what else is there to be,
At seventeen?

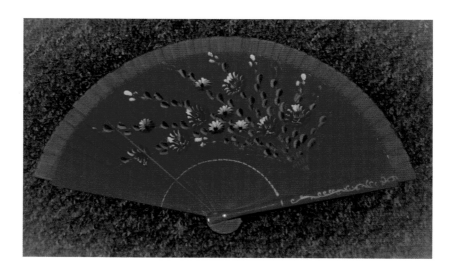

White Rain

The start of the ball, my debutante night, presented to the queen
in state.
Spied from the stairs, the ladies of the dance trilling, bidding
their wares for a dance's calling card.
Showers of pearl and lace float upon clouds of tulle, debutante
and dandy guess at meaning,
Hesitation and trepidation in society's marriage market hall.
The wary captured in pearled starlight as a confetti of fans
shower hope and fear across the dance floor.

The start of my life, my debutante night,
The start of my life, a rain of white.

Should I be scared, nervous?
My stomach would be chittering at the thought of tonight if it
weren't for the stomacher laced tight.
The straits of whalebone hold me upright, rigid and poised as I
await my mother to chaperone and present me to the Queen.

I must appear calmer than I seem, it would not do to seem
skittish; I anxiously tap my fan in my palm, fritter the time
Until I must glide nymph-like towards that discerning stare.

It's no use my ladies telling me that this is a special night, that
one night, when the glance of love may just alight upon my life;
I am scared, nervous, of not doing it right.
What if I don't like the matches on offer tonight? Do I have a
say, a right?

I hold to the faith that it will be alright, that mother and father
met on such a night and are together still.
But I cannot quiet the disquiet that jangles along my nerves,
cannot unhear the quarrels I've heard on late nights.
My life is held in abeyance on the whim of a fan it would seem.

Cupid's Messenger

Fretted ivory blades like frozen lace, shatters looks in crocheted
　　ivory and exotic mother-of-pearl.
Ribbons, jewels, festooned as a boon to the panoply of society
　　and conversation,
Frippery behind screens of false smiles and marriage bartering.

She rests folded paper against her lips: 'I don't trust you',
Reinforces the message with a slow fanning: 'Don't waste your
　　time, I don't care about you'.
This paramour, elegance defined in finery and pearl,
Has no heart to cut me so with slices of air across the room.

Troubadours of Dance

The flick of the wrist called, and dismissed the shadows,
Lace edges veiling desire, watchers of the fringes.
Ephemeral butterflies cocooned in vagaries of history and
  societal etiquette, dainty feminine weapons holding charm
  and disgust by the simple turn of a palm.
Such fashionable devices of practicality and beauty combine as
  we dine once more
From the dance floor.

Gallanting a Fan

She smiles behind the painted veil, both coy and brave.
A breath of wind; the promise of a spoken word hushed.

He nods, a slow turn of the head, strong; this is how we behave.
This is how we shall dance, weave invisible threads across the
  room to catch love's muse.

Half-opened, her fan rests across a delicate face: 'We are being
  watched over'. Her gaze is steadfast, yet chaste.

His smile remains, the match is made, the thread is caught and
  woven.

She folds her fan, it rests, an edge kissing the corner of her right
  eye—"When may I be allowed to see you?"

The weave shuttles back and forth, a dance is called, her card
  has his mark.
A breath is caught upon her ear, curls into her heart, and
  blooms.

Discourse

I will talk to you.
This is my language, the language of fans,
This is the discussion you will learn.

My face, my beauty, in your hand,
Your (my) story, your (my) truth,
Will be told.

To another across the floor, fan yourself quickly, and I will tell
him you love him so much.
Fold me across your heart, and he will know your heart breaks
with the depth of love within, that your love for him makes
you suffer and pine.
Drop me (but don't forget to retrieve me) and he will know you
belong only to him.

Be coy, examine my sheaves, look closely at my painting. He
will know your intent, that you're interested in him.
If a stronger desire you want portrayed, then hide your eyes
behind me.
Draw me across your cheek, slowly, tell him you love him,
But don't mistake this with the hatred displayed when drawing
my handle through your hand.

Rest me on your right cheek, say 'yes',
On the left for 'no'.
Rest my handle upon your lips to taste his sweet kiss.

Look at him and close me, 'I wish to speak with you'.
Open me wide, 'Wait for me'.
Place me behind your head with a finger extended, "Goodbye."

contd…

Carrying me in your right hand, held in front of your face,
'Follow me'.

He will keep a secret for you if you cover your left ear with an
open fan,
And accept your apology when you pull me slowly across your
eyes.

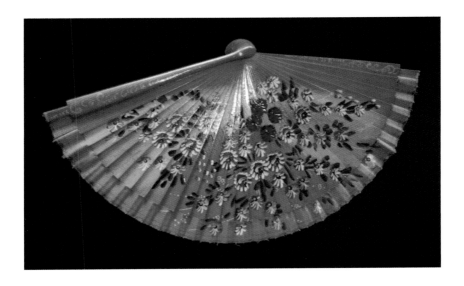

I will talk to you.
This is my language, the language of fans,
To survive, this is the discussion you must learn.

Dowager

I spy from my town house window as carriages line up at St James Palace, awaiting their presentation. I see the watchful eyes alight upon silk court gowns and pearled tiaras, feather and lace fans held tenderly in gloved hands.

That was me, so long ago. That was me.

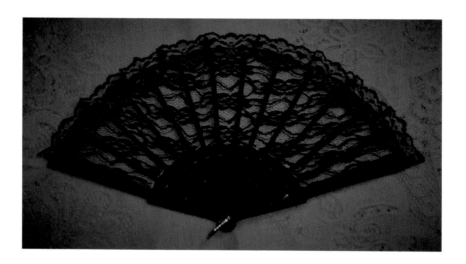

Their schooling shows in their deportment, the import of an elegant, poised and beautiful life, a far cry from the fields and winnowing fans of farmers and their daughters. These young ladies bred for the marriage market, a bartering of society.

That was me, so long ago. That was me.

contd...

I spy those that jumped up their station, the common girls from country dances, where the beautiful seek wealthy patronage, spinster or dowager to call the hackney for a season of dances; where common families seek matches among the eligible of London Town; where jealous fillies at debutante balls wish the match was theirs.

That was me, so long ago. That was me.

I am that dowager, my patronage on offer for the bid of beauty and charm. Nostalgia folded in my hand, a fan of pearl and turquoise parchment, a masque against the tiredness of time.

That was me, so long ago. That was me.

Miscellany and Glossary

During my research, I discovered a plethora of history of information, and interestingly so many fans have their own names. Here are but a few that fascinated me:

Alphabet	painted with simple lessons for teaching children.
Bridal fan	a gift from a groom to his bride.
Brisé	fan with no leaf, sticks held in place by ribbons.
Chicken-skin	this sounds horrific! Leaves made from skin taken from an unborn kid, dressed and treated; results in leaves with a very fine grain; 17th century onwards. Swan's skins have also been used in some parts of Europe (there is one in the museum of Krakow).
Dagger fan	the handle withdraws and turns into a lethal dagger. Made in Japan and Italy (where they used stiletto blades).
Domino	a fan with two cut out sections for eyes to be used as a mask, painted to look like velvet or lace. Used in masquerade balls.
Gumbai uchiwa	flat iron Japanese battle fans 11th-12th century. Leaf is double, of painted leather, with an iron handle, around 40cms, painted and bound with a long cord and tassel.
Gun sen	folding iron Japanese battle fan, 12th-20th century.
Lorgnette	popularised by Madame du Barry (mistress of Louis XV, 1743-1793), having a lorgnette (opera glasses) concealed in the sticks or handle.

39

Kanasawa	special 19th century fan made for a man, highly prized, created in Kanasawa, on the west coast of Japan.
Kyoto	an etched fan, made in Kyoto, Japan, with copperplate engraving.
Mai ogi	Japanese dancing fans; 17th-18th century
Mica	mineral of a foliated structure consisting of thin laminae or scales, dug from mines and found in volcanic areas. Used to decorate fans as small, almost transparent panels. The Messel Mica fan is one of only four surviving fans of its type (European made) known to be in existence.
Mita ogi	giant Japanese processional fan, around 2m long.
Ripidium	fixed religious fans, often in silver, still seen in Greece.

Acknowledgements:

The history of fans (Nancy Armstrong)
Snow Flower and the Secret Fan (Lisa See)
V&A Museum, London
The Hive, Worcester
Guild of Fan Makers
The Fan Museum, Greenwich
The Fitzwilliam Museum, Cambridge

About the Author

Leena Batchelor is a Worcester-based poet and spoken word artist, Worcestershire Poet Laureate 2020-21 and Poet-in-Residence for The Commandery, Worcester.

Her poems have featured in several anthologies, and she currently has three solo poetry collections, with themes ranging from war, politics, life and love.

Calling herself a 'poetic minstrel with living in her veins', Leena finds her inspiration in her many travels around the UK and watching life whilst sipping over the rim of a teacup and writes passionately about subjects that strike her mind and heart.

Leena also provides talks and workshops on how poetry is a valuable tool for everyday life and an antidote to the vitriolic rhetoric pervading society. She uses poetry as a medium to support and raise funds for several charities, including mental health and the armed forces.

For details of Leena's collections and contact information, visit her website: www.pixiemuse.wordpress.com

To listen to Leena's readings and watch recorded performances, visit her YouTube channel: PixieMuse Poetry & Prose.

Leena can also be found on Facebook (PixieMuse Poetry & Prose), Twitter (@pixie_dragonfly) and Instagram (pixiemusepoetry).

Endorsements

I have seen and been addicted to her work. Beautifully descriptive and powerful with imagery so lucid you can see her stories unfold in front of your eyes like a movie.
Georgie Bull—Fiction Fridays

A fascinating panorama of fan history—readers will be intrigued by the diversity Leena discovers in the subject. She plays effortlessly with a broad variety of voices, both historical and personal, and spices it all up with vivid description.
Jeff Cottrill—Journalist and Performance Poet

From Chinese silk through to Victorian lace, from Elizabethan Queens to scandalous provocations at the Moulin Rouge, Leena Batchelor, in between intimate memories of dressing-up amid her grandmother's belongings, takes us on a journey through a sumptuous world of folded fabrics opening with the intent of sharing secrets, a panoply of poetry perfectly curated like these object d'art that have been held by history. A de rigueur debut poetry collection for all those who appreciate attention to the most delicate detail. A history lesson in itself touching on samurai swords, ivory blades, sworn sisters and delicate debutants catching blushed breaths behind the only armour they had at hand; the single unfolding of a fan. 'This is my language, my language of fans,' we are told, and we settle down, without a flicker of hesitation, swept from car to carriage and across the centuries.
Damien Donnelly—Author and Podcaster